T0161128

CHOICES

POEMS OF
LIFE AND LOVE

KATHRYN CAROLE ELLISON

Published by Lady Bug Books, an imprint of Brisance Books Group.
Lady Bug Press and the distinctive ladybug logo are registered trademarks of
Lady Bug Books, LLC.

Lady Bug Books
400 112th Avenue N.E.
Suite 230
Bellevue, WA 98004
www.GiftsOfLove.com

For information about custom editions, special sales and permissions, please email
Info@GiftsOfLove.com

Manufactured in the United States of America
ISBN: 978-1-944194-92-5

First Edition: September 2023

A NOTE FROM THE AUTHOR

The poems in this book were written over many years as gifts to my children. I began writing them in the 1970s, when they were reaching the age of reason. As I found myself in the position of becoming a single parent, I wanted to do something special to share with them – something that would become a tradition, a ritual they could count on.

And so the Advent Poems began – one day, decades ago – with a poem 'gifted' to them each day during the Advent period leading up to Christmas, December 1 to December 24. Nearly fifty years later, my kids still look forward each year to the 'gifted' poems that continue a family tradition, and that new generations have come to cherish.

It is my sincere hope that you will embrace and enjoy them and share them with those you love.

Children of the Light was among the early poems I wrote, and is included in each of the *Poems of Life and Love* books in The Ellison Collection: (alphabetically) *Awakenings, Beginnings, Celebrations, Choices, Conversations, Gratitude, Happiness, Heartstrings, Horizons, Inspirations, Milestones, Mindfulness, Moments, Possibilities, Reflections, Sanctuary, Sojourns,* and *Tapestry.*

After writing many hundreds of poems, *Children of the Light* is still my favorite. In the process of writing it, the words seemed to spring from my heart, and soul… and flowed so effortlessly that it was written in a single sitting. All I needed to do was capture the words on paper.

"Light," to me represents all that is good and pure and right with the world, and I believed then – as I do today – that those elements live in my children, and in all of us.

We need only to dare.

– KCE

DEDICATION

To My Parents: Herb and Bernice Haas

Mom, you were the poet who went before me.
Thanks for paving the way.
From you I learned to appreciate the power of Poetry.

And Dad (Daddy), you always believed in me,
no matter what direction my life took.
Thank you for your faith in me,
and for your unconditional love.

Table of contents

Life's joys

NEW BEGINNINGS	3
BE THE SOLUTION	5
SUPER POWERS	7
TRANSFORMATION	8
WORDS	9
TEARS ARE THE ELIXIR OF RECOVERY	10
WHEN THE GOING GETS ROUGH	11
RISK	13
LOVE OR FEAR	14
A SENSE OF WONDER	15
CHANGE	17
BECAUSE YOU HAVE A CHOICE, YOU HAVE A CHANCE	19
ACCEPTANCE: THE FIFTH STAGE	21

Life's lessons

THE CHOICE IS YOURS TO MAKE	25
COURAGE	27
WORK ETHIC	28
FREEDOM OF RESPONSIBILITY	29

YOU LIVE AND YOU DIE BY THE
CHOICES YOU MAKE   31
BE THE LIGHT   33
THE BIRTHRIGHT   35
COURTESY   36
ORIGINALITY   37
TRUST THE VOICE WITHIN   39
ENEMIES   40
DO YOUR BEST, FORGET THE REST   41
HIDE AND SEEK   42
STAND UP   43
CHILDREN OF THE LIGHT   45

LIFE'S GIFTS

SUCCESS   49
UP IN THE AIR   50
CONSIDER WHAT COMES FIRST   51
ADAPTABILITY   53
VISION   55
COMMITMENT   56
MORE PROACTIVITY   57
WRITE YOUR OWN SCRIPT   59
HESITATION   60
THE INEVITABILITY OF CHANGE   61
WILLIAM JAMES, YOU ARE SO WISE   63

LIFE'S JOYS

NEW BEGINNINGS

How lovely it is to know that tomorrow
Is a new day for you... with yet no mistakes;
To have something so clean and fresh to look forward to
Gives you hope for your future, for goodness sakes!

In fact, every moment is a fresh beginning.
Start right now, don't wait for tomorrow.
Your life does not get better by chance;
It gets better by change... lose your sorrow.

"The only person you are destined to become
Is the person you decide to be."
Emerson shared this bit of wisdom;
His message is simple... I'm sure you'll agree.

Be willing to get rid of the life you planned
In order to receive your life in the waiting.
You must shed the old skin, be open to change.
With new attitudes, a new life you're creating.

Holding on is believing that there's only the past.
Letting go is knowing that there's a future for you.
It all begins in the beginning, as you know;
And it begins after you shift your mind… it's true!

Stop being afraid of what could go wrong.
Concentrate on all that will go right.
As Dolly Parton says, "If you don't like the road,
Start paving another one." (Such insight!)

Buddha shared wisdom about new beginnings.
His words are soothing; they have much to say.
"Each morning… we are born again.
It matters most what we do today."

BE THE SOLUTION

Did you know? There is a direct correlation
Between positive energy and a positive result!
In order to attract positive things in your life,
Give off positive energy. It's not difficult.

Only give out what you want to get back,
And don't use your energy to worry!
Worry's a negative message to the universe.
At best, results will be blurry.

When you seem to reach bottom with a negative outlook...
When you say, "It can't get any worse..."
You are challenging the universe to do exactly that!
You are part of the problem. Put things in reverse.
Wayne Dyer's words, when he shared this thought,
Had a logic to them. They did not seem strange.
"Change the way you look at things, my friends,
And the things you look at will change."

Let's turn now to the words of our own Bill Gates...
A redirection from the negative to the positive tense;
"Spend more time and energy supporting what you favor
Than opposing what you're [absolutely] against."

With positive energy, you can expect positive outcomes.
(Your positivity to others heals your own pain.)
Sometimes your joy is the source of your smile,
And the opposite is true – the message is plain.
Your smile can be the source of your joy.
It's a wonderful lesson – to trick your own brain!

Take responsibility for the energy that you bring,
And choose wisely the things you do with your time.
You create your own reality – there's no fine print...
No exceptions... no asterisks. The right choice is sublime.

SUPER POWERS

Okay, so admit it... at some point in time
You've tried to see if you had super powers!
Moving a pencil with your mind, or bending a spoon,
You've spent time in practice – maybe long hours!

We all wish that we had great super powers.
We wish we could do more than we can do.
Well, there are many varieties of super powers,
And we possess them already! (Who knew?)

By listening to your own inner voices so loud...
And trusting your own super powers that appear,
You stand up to the villain that dwells within.
You concentrate on your strengths and lose the fear.

Strengths, not weaknesses; and powers, not problems...
All the powers of the universe have been given to you.
Live each day as if you know you've been given
Super powers to succeed at everything you do.

TRANSFORMATION

Real transformation requires real honesty, and
No longer fooling yourself about the job at hand.
Transformation is more about unlearning than learning;
And it begins now, not later, you understand.

You never change things by fighting what exists.
No, you build something new; what exists is made obsolete.
Change is inevitable; transformation is by conscious choice.
Letting go of the familiar puts you in the driver's seat.

"If you change the way you look at things,
The things you are looking at will change."
Wayne Dyer shared the above bit of wisdom...
His logic, once understood, does not seem strange.

Change does not come from an outside source;
No, change begins with the person at the center.
That's you, of course... no other person could it be.
You either allow for transformation, or you're the preventer.

WORDS

That book of Noah Webster is filled with words.
They are listed from A to Z.
The words by themselves are harmless enough,
But meaning comes from usage, don't you see?

Words can take us to heaven or to hell,
Depending on their use in the conversation.
Words of a lullaby can put a baby to sleep,
And words of hatred can halt communication.

Words can start a war or they can keep the peace.
It's to one's advantage to select them well;
And arrange them to inspire the minds others
So that in their lives the joy of living will dwell.

Words of faith, hope and courage lift men ever upward.
Negative words have the heinous power to destroy.
Choose well your words. They follow you always.
In your future you'll reap either sorrow or joy.

TEARS ARE THE ELIXIR OF RECOVERY

Every time a choice is made a leaf must fall,
Not to be attached as nature would intend.
It's said we die a little when we make a choice,
And with a loss it's only natural to grieve.
Tears of pain or of remorse are what we get –
An elixir – to cleanse and heal the wounds we suffer.
The tears cleanse the panes through which we look
And clearer vision is the consequence of tears.

WHEN THE GOING GETS ROUGH

Sometimes when the going gets kind of rough
You begin to wonder why
You chose this task to do at this time.
You're struggling so hard, you could cry...

Just pause for a moment, I beseech,
And check the purpose behind it.
If you are doing what you believe
Your course is pure, and you won't mind it.

It's when you work hard for what you believe
That the fruits of your labor are divine.
Because you're putting yourself out there;
Your whole being is on the line.

To dare to risk you must believe
In yourself and in your choice.
God wants only good for you.
He wants you to rejoice!

He wants you to know true self-respect,
To be able to say, "Look at me!"
He wants you to preside over your own fan club;
He wants you to live life with glee!

Just knowing all this, your struggle will lessen,
And what was once a heavy load
Becomes rather light and easy to carry
As you journey on down the road.

RISK

Risk is defined as a possibility of loss;
Or suffering harm as a result of a choice.
The list of synonyms fill up a page.
One funny man described it in this voice:
"Risk is like playing with a chemistry set
Without reading the directions beforehand."
Our lives **do** change as we encounter new challenges.
There **are** elements of risk, you understand.

"Dancing on the razor's edge," or "leaping into the dark,"
"Playing with fire" or "Russian roulette;"
"Take a chance," "run a risk," and "go for broke" –
The descriptions all quite graphic in the color palette.

The day might come when a change takes place
And the risk to remain tightly closed in a bud
Will be more painful than the risk to bloom.
For Anais Nin it was true. (Change came in a flood!)
Every change is a challenge – a risk to grow,
To become authentically expert.
With both grief and celebration you move to a new stage.
Know that who you really are cannot be hurt.

LOVE OR FEAR

They cannot be experienced at the same time;
It's either one or the other.
Love makes your life just next to sublime,
And fear is always a bother.

The ego mind saves up old hurts –
Old memories from the past.
It fools us into thinking they matter,
That they are meant to last.

Stop running the old painful tapes –
They're holding you back, my dear.
Remember the title of that now famous book:
LOVE IS LETTING GO OF FEAR.

A SENSE OF WONDER

From birth, a child is bombarded by experiences
That instill a sense of wonder quite profound.
According to Socrates, wonder is the beginning of wisdom, and
Nature is the first place a sense of wonder is found.

Dew on a spider's web; a robin building its nest...
A dog licking an ice cream cone in the park...
Discovering the world around him, the child begins
His journey to make his own mark.

What is grand about childhood? Everything is a wonder!
It is not merely a miracle-filled world.
Oh no, quite the opposite! With wonder at every turn,
It is a miraculous world to be discovered and unfurled.

Human growth has no limits; its boundaries are infinite!
Intelligence, imagination and wonder are the guides.
By looking at everything as if you are seeing it anew,
You'll not lose your sense of wonder. In you it resides.

People love to wonder, and that's the seed of science.
We've been to the moon and back, and then beyond!
We've improved medicine and agriculture; people live longer lives.
To the miracles in our lives we are happy to respond.

There's so much to see – there's so much to learn;
Our time here on earth is brief.
I would rather have a mind that is opened by wonder
Than one that is closed by belief!

CHANGE

Other people can make me crazy;
Other people can do me wrong;
I can't change them, don't you know,
So why not just sing a song?

CHORUS:
It's not you – it's me
That's in for some changes.
It's not you – you see;
My attitude rearranges.
I can't change anything
Except my own view.
And that is the answer.
It's me – not you.

I can't change the world;
I can't even change my history;
I can't change them, don't you know.
That's what makes it such a mystery.

CHORUS:

I can't change other people
Even if they're wrong,
So I might as well relax
And just sing my song.

CHORUS:

I can't always change what happens
Around my outside being,
But I can change me inside
And the view I am seeing.

CHORUS:

BECAUSE YOU HAVE A CHOICE, YOU HAVE A CHANCE

According to William Jennings Bryan
Your destiny is a matter of choice.
It's a thing to be achieved, and when it is
You have many reasons to rejoice.

You can be miserable, to be sure,
Or you can be happily self-motivated.
The ball is in your court (isn't it always?).
Your choices are yours to be activated.

The decisions you make are a choice of values.
They reflect your life in every way.
It is these decisions that shape your path.
Make good choices for yourself every day.

Every choice you make has an end result.
Making good ones will afford you a chance
To better opportunities and a happier life,
As along life's trail you advance.

With good choices come opportunities – chances –
To improve your situation... to make your life better.
Your chances of success can always be measured
By your belief in yourself... be a go-getter!

ACCEPTANCE: THE FIFTH STAGE

Denial, anger, bargaining, depression, and acceptance:
The stages that happen in learning to live with loss.
Whether loss of a loved one or losing a job,
These tools help us frame our feelings without the chaos.

Acceptance does not mean you feel complete resignation.
Resigning to something without moving forward doesn't fit.
Acceptance means understanding a real situation,
And knowing there's a way for you to move through it.

Happiness grows in proportion to your acceptance,
And in inverse proportion to your expectation.
Accepting things that happen as they are
Will give you clarity of mind for observation.

With danger, panic causes tunnel vision.
It dampens your ability to see an alternative.
Calm acceptance allows you to evaluate,
And move in a direction that's affirmative.

LIFE'S LESSONS

THE CHOICE IS YOURS TO MAKE

Jean-Paul Sartre says that "We are our choices."
Well now, do you agree or not?
If you've ever wondered who you are in this world,
Then Sartre's statement may be your best shot.

Your beliefs are your choice... a statement bold.
You are prompted to act, based on your own inner voices.
"First you choose your beliefs (It's your life, after all.)."
And these beliefs affect your choices.

The choices you make today shape the person you'll become.
Base them on your hopes, not fears, as you go.
Your choices show what you are, more than your abilities.
Choose wisely, and watch your confidence grow.

It's not hard to make decisions if you know your own values,
And always be ready to experience the consequences.
Every choice you make has an end result.
Right decisions, by you, measure your competence.

Happiness is a choice. We can choose to be happy.
If we have too many lemons we can make lemonade,
Wayne Dyer confirms this idea in his "take" on the subject:
"Our lives are the sum total of the choices we have made."

COURAGE

Courage is not the absence of fear,
As many people might say...
No, it's your triumph over it
That will always save the day.

Churchill implied courage takes more than one form:
[It's] "what it takes to stand up and speak."
And also, [It] "takes courage to sit down and listen."
Hearing the other side does not make you weak.

Taking the risk of going too far
Helps to establish how far you can go.
Do not let your actions be influenced by your fears.
Fears get in the way of your innate "mojo."

Courage is contagious... in the very best way.
You admire someone who takes a strong stand.
When a brave man does this, you will often notice
The spines of those around him will stiffen and expand.

WORK ETHIC

What you do in this world is what matters,
Not what you think, say, or plan.
If there's something you think you cannot do,
Then, for heaven's sake, do what you can!

Who you are tomorrow always begins
With what you are doing today.
The harder you work, the luckier you get.
Love what you are doing and work becomes play.

Nothing can bring you success but yourself.
Hard work works harder than luck.
Work ethic is a choice. It's not a talent;
And success comes from "walking your talk."

If you want true and lasting success,
Surround yourself with people of integrity.
Deliver more than you promise, and earn their respect.
You'll carry your head high, and with dignity.

FREEDOM OF RESPONSIBILITY

Imagine that there are two kinds of courage:
One is active and gets people killed;
The other is inner and keeps people alive.
Which of these is better?

Remember, no one can answer for you,
For each kind of courage has its pros and cons.
Questions like these you alone must answer.
What do you think?

Keep in mind that Tao means now,
Tao means only how things happen.
It's not the same as what-I-should-do.
Isn't that up to you?

No one can tell you what to do,
Though you may think others have your answers.
It's your responsibility alone.
Are you willing to try?

CHOICES

Instead of asking for advice
Learn to be more aware of what's happening.
Then you'll be able to see for yourself:
"What is going on?"

Armed with awareness, your decisions become easy
About what is the right thing to do.
You can make good decisions if you are alert.
Isn't it nice to know?

What you do is your own responsibility.
Tao does not dictate behavior.
But your patterns follow Natural Law...
Did you know that?

The freedom of responsibility
Does not mean you don't have to think.
It means you must decide for yourself:
What is your destiny?

YOU LIVE AND YOU DIE BY THE CHOICES YOU MAKE

Your life is the sum total of the choices you make.
You choose the directions that your life will take.
You decide what you want, you hold the wheel,
So steer your course and your life will reveal
The results of your choices. It's always your move.
As it unfolds, you look to improve.

It's your choices that show what you really are –
More than your abilities – oh man, by far!
You are solely responsible for the actions you choose.
You must accept the consequences and risk the blues.
In deeds, words and thoughts throughout your lifetime,
Your awareness to detail must work all the time.

Mankind's greatest gift, or course, if you will –
Is that we have free choice, and it takes skill
To determine the motive for the choices as they appear.
Make sure they're based on love, not fear.
Sometimes it's only a choice of attitude,
And sometimes it will result in gratitude.

CHOICES

The key to your universe? Your ability to choose!
It's very important and nothing to abuse.
Only by exercising your choosing right
Can you exercise the ability to change your plight.
And accidental choices are as important (yours and mine)
As the careful choices you make by design.

Other people's choices are nothing more
Than another alternative for you to explore.
You may make a thousand little choices each day;
All of them count as you walk your pathway.
Some of your choices may cause you strife,
So, manage your choices and you'll manage your life.

The end result of your life on this planet
Will be the sum total of your choices. You plan it.
Freedom comes to you when that power you keep:
The power to choose. You sow and you reap.
Make good decisions and in them rejoice.
There's no life as complete as the life lived by choice.

BE THE LIGHT

Leonard Cohen says, 'There's a crack in everything,
And that's how the light gets in.'
A quick and humorous explanation, it is,
And one that brings on a grin...

But think of the concepts 'light' and 'darkness,'
And what they mean in discussion.
They are opposite sides of the same coin:
One brightens, one darkens... a comparison.

'Light is to darkness what love is to fear...
In the presence of one, the other disappears.'
Marianne Williamson is credited with the above quote.
Positive thinking can chase away the fears.

As your light shines, others around you can see.
Your act gives them permission to shine the same.
And, as you work to create light for others
You naturally light your own way… it's a game.

Knowing there's light is one thing…
Being the light is even more.
It takes courage to be able to see it…
Passing it on raises the score.

THE BIRTHRIGHT

Ownership of who you are and of what you do
Is a birthright that is yours and yours alone...
With it, a guarantee that is carved in stone.
The right to live your life you can pursue.

Each one of us holds power that's within
To become who we wish in thought and deed.
To find it is a joy, it is agreed.
The birthright, all along, has been built in.

Resolve to find yourself by taking hold
Of the birthright that lives within us all,
And hear the misery thunder in its fall
As you progress in line with movement bold.

COURTESY

Those who sow courtesy reap friendship,
And those who plant kindness gather love.
Gratitude is the most exquisite form of courtesy.
It costs nothing, and buys everything! A joy, thereof.

When restraint and courtesy are added to strength,
The latter becomes resistible to any deterrence.
Courtesy opens doors, it straightens the road
On a friendlier path to victory. There's no interference.

Passion and courtesy are two polar opposites,
But serve to balance each other to a full-blooded whole.
Socialization (courtesy) tempers the overbearing passion,
And drive (or passion) moves things to your desired goal.

Allow passion and courtesy into your lives each day
In equal measure for balance of purpose.
Courtesy and courage are needed daily
To keep life humming along with a positive focus.

ORIGINALITY

I've heard it said many times in my life,
With varying volumes of expression,
As I have tried to come up with an original thought:
"There is nothing that is new under the sun."

C. S. Lewis related that telling the truth,
Whether it had been told before or not,
Was the key to approaching originality.
The truth you should never boycott.

Originality implies being bold enough
To go beyond accepted norms.
Who decides what's acceptable, anyway?
What about truth? There's only one form.

Original or Authentic? Oh my, what a choice!
Some people say originality does not exist!
Select things or thoughts that speak directly to your soul,
Then extend them to the limits, and be the artist!

Don't try to be original; just share your own truth.
Find your voice in whatever moves your soul.
It takes courage to pay attention to the sound of your own voice.
Tell the truth, and you will have found your role.

Be creative! It's contagious! Surround yourself with others
Who look to solve problems by thinking anew.
It's way more fun; your life will be happier!
You're on your way to becoming an 'original you!'

TRUST THE VOICE WITHIN

We must trust that voice within our hearts
That tells us what's in store for us each day.
All the wisdom that we need is there
To dance with joy on life's highway.

There is no time that we should feel at odds
About which steps to take and when to take them.
To make the choices that are best for us,
We simply hear with an inner listening system.

Each of us is guided by a voice
That we can choose to tune in when we want.
Its frequency is strong, we turn the dial
And synchronize with what is relevant.

ENEMIES

You've got enemies? That's good!
It means you stood up for what you believe!
Your enemies force out the best in you
As you set out on your path to achieve.

Quite often your own worst enemy
Is the one between your ears.
Negative thoughts will hold you back,
And leave you trembling in fear.

Wish your enemies a long life, so they can see your success
(Unkind people need your kindness the most.)
Forgive them, but do not forget their names.
In your endeavor you must stay engrossed.

Oscar Wilde taught us to forgive our enemies.
Sometimes that is difficult to do.
He says, "...nothing [can] annoy them so much."
Stay on your path. The onus is on you.

DO YOUR BEST, FORGET THE REST

Yes, the title rhymes to catch your eye,
And the message is one of importance.
If, at the end of your day, you're unhappy,
Perhaps you've not gone "the distance."

Doing your best each moment of the day
Guarantees your contentment at its close.
Doing your best each moment will put you
In the best place for the next one, I disclose.

Doing your best is like planting a seed.
What you plant now, you will harvest later.
Don't compare your best to anyone else's.
Improve what you're doing. Make it greater!

Wake up each day and ask yourself,
"How best can I use today's time?"
Your success isn't measured by what you've accomplished,
But by how much you valued it, meantime.

HIDE AND SEEK

The ego can fool us into faulty thinking.
It hides from us the Love that resides within,
So we look outside to seek it where we can.
Of course, we never find it, though we search.
And all the time it's there within our reach,
Closer than our ego would let us know.

We do not have to accept there's a lack of Love.
It's there within us, ready to be tapped.
Our spirits can soar because of all the Love –
We simply have to choose to look within.
Be willing first to choose, and then it happens.
The Love within us is in our hands and hearts.

STAND UP

It takes courage to stand up for what you believe,
To be true and honest and right!
Yet, it is said that if you don't stand up.
Wrong will win out, without a fight.

Have the courage to say "No!"
Have the courage to face the truth.
Do the right thing because it is right!
Living your life with integrity takes work,
But do it! Do it with all of your might!

It is said that if you don't stand for something
You'll fall for anything that sounds true;
But a wise person proportions his belief to the evidence.
Check your sources, do your homework, take the long view.

In politics, if a party stands for nothing but reelection,
Then it indeed stands for nothing worth much.
The world suffers a lot because of the silence
Of the good people who use timidness as a crutch.

CHOICES

Our lives begin to end the day we become silent
About things that matter to us, and to the planet.
We might place ourselves in danger when we stand,
But place our children in greater danger when we don't.

Oh, one more thing about taking a stand:
Be polite, don't raise your voice, be firm.
Remember, what you believe will depend on what you are.
Let people know, and if need be, reconfirm.

CHILDREN OF THE LIGHT

There are those souls who bring the light,
Who spill it out for all to share.
And with a joy that does excite,
They show the world that they do care.
It is so very bright.

In this sharing, love does pervade
Into their lives and cycles round;
And as this light is outward played
The love is also inward bound.
It is an awesome trade.

You are a soul whose light is shared.
It comes from deep within your heart.
It's best because it is not spared,
Because it's total, not just part.
And I am glad you've dared.

LIFE'S GIFTS

SUCCESS

Success in life, in love, in work,
Is a positive and happy outcome.
So why do we approach success in things
With negative "What ifs?" Is that dumb?

Be solution oriented, don't think in terms
Of the scope or of the seriousness of the riddle.
Acknowledge the need to solve it now;
Make a move, don't stay in the middle.

Have faith that inside every problem
Lies an inherent solution to unravel.
Seek counsel from others, but don't forget
To close your eyes, and inwardly travel.

Face your trials cheerfully, don't hide from them.
They're like barking dogs who chase if you run.
Confronted, they're forced to recede until
You've solved them all – every one.

UP IN THE AIR

Being up in the air gives a person a "lift."
(Then the wondering sets in where to land...)
Use the time to advantage when you're cast adrift;
Make sure you don't fall in quicksand.

When you're up in the air, it means you've let go
Of an old situation. That's good!
A change is in order, you've told yourself so,
But direction may not be understood.

It's okay to be floating while making your choices.
You've more freedom to pursue those of interest.
You're pulled this way and that by capricious winds
Until you make the choice that is best.

And when you alight from that free flight above,
Your goals more firmly in mind...
You'll pursue with vigor a path you will love;
And your fortune, indeed, you will find.

CONSIDER WHAT COMES FIRST

Before undertaking a prospective action...
To avoid an accident... (you could end up in traction),
Step back and take a very long look
At the entire picture. (Don't take the "hook.")

Acting rashly on raw impulse is not the way
To succeed in pursuing your goals, I dare say.
To think about what happens first, then the next phase,
Should be studied before jumping in, eyes aglaze.

After study is over, and if appropriate, take action
Based on what you've learned to your satisfaction.
Often, one jumps in without circumspection
And the result is retreat, regret and rejection.

Consider the big picture and don't be a dabbler
(A person who plays only as long as it's comfortable).
To play at something is not the real deal.
It's play acting, not committing, and has no appeal.

Unless you fully give yourself over
To each and every personal endeavor
You're pretending; you're a mimic, and superficial.
And any reward would seem artificial.

A halfhearted spirit has no power.
A tentative effort and the deal turns sour.
Consider first the nature of your intent,
Then measure that against how you are competent.

ADAPTABILITY

Have you noticed that life doesn't always stay the same?
And have you noticed that in order to survive,
Your ability to adapt plays an all-important role?
(It's a skill worth having if you want to stay alive.)

Darwin said survival of the species depends upon
The ability to adapt to change (which can be difficult to foresee).
Remember, change is the constant. (It's the only thing that is.)
Strength or intelligence, alone, is no guarantee.

A humorist by the name of Anon Y. Mous
Once made this statement (now, please don't yawn):
"When something goes wrong in your life (and it will)
Just yell, 'Plot Twist!!' Regroup. And move on.

There's honesty in humor, quite often, because
It eases your move into 'truth' with less pain.
Adapting to change requires flexibility,
And a dose of humility – creativity to attain.

It can be said that all failure in your life
Is failure to adapt to the change that is occurring.
Adaptability is the simple secret of survival.
This I believe, and surely you're concurring.

VISION

Sight is what your eyes produce
And vision is sourced from the heart.
So, never let what your eyes can see
Affect your vision. Know them apart.

Vision is more than seeing what can be...
It's an appeal to your better qualities.
It's a call to be something more than you are...
An opportunity to reach your potentialities.

Vision with action can change the world!
This life is your one chance to reach your goal!
Don't let fear or doubt keep you from accomplishing;
Keep moving forward... you are in control.

Without vision of your future you'll return to your past.
Your reality will be determined by outdated perceptions.
Oh, and always chase your vision, not the money...
Money will follow, with few exceptions.

COMMITMENT

The quality of people's lives, I've been told,
Is in direct proportion to their commitment to excellence.
Their chosen field of endeavor doesn't matter.
Success is usually guaranteed, once they commence.

It was character that first got you out of bed,
And commitment that moved you into action.
Discipline enabled you to follow through,
And finish the job with satisfaction.

Commitment is an act, and not just a word.
You need discipline and hard work to get you there.
That's called follow-through – you roll up your sleeves,
And put your best foot forward, with care.

The only limit to your impact, my loves,
Is your imagination and commitment to your goal.
Without commitment there are only promises and hopes,
But no plans… so, make them. You are in control.

MORE PROACTIVITY

Reactive people only feel safe
When others treat them well.
When people don't, they are protective,
And live in a defensive hell.

They are driven by feelings and by conditions
Which affect them and their surroundings.
They are at the mercy of outside things,
And often take brutal poundings.

Proactive people, on the other hand,
Are driven by deliberate values.
Their values are carefully thought about,
Then lived by in all their venues.

Don't get this wrong, don't think for a minute
That proactive people are immune
To external stimuli from every corner.
They just don't let them play their "tune."

Remember, it is our willing permission,
Our consent to what happens to us,
That hurts us more than the event itself.
Any other explanation is bogus.

Until a person can say honestly,
"I am what I am today
Because of the choices I made before,"
He cannot choose another way.

WRITE YOUR OWN SCRIPT

Ask yourself this question, my loves
(With the answer you'll be well-equipped):
"Am I spending my time doing what I alone
Would write into my life's script?"

You must take control of the words in your head.
(They are yours from your inner perceptions.)
When you write them from a positive point of view,
You'll have more meaningful conceptions.

You'll be able to produce the experience you want...
Not some mild, watered-down version.
You'll create a momentum that allows you to do
What you value and love, with immersion.

You'll write your own lines and direct the production,
And you'll delight in the ease of the flow.
When you have the right script for directing your life,
You'll always be the star of the show.

HESITATION

Most hesitation in human interaction
Is caused by doubt or fear... or both.
By taking a deep breath and plunging forward
You will follow your instincts... to growth!

A moment of hesitation may cause a lifetime of regrets.
Hesitation is often a mistake that invites defeat.
Make up your mind to act in a decided manner.
You've done the thinking... now, jump in! Compete!

Fear causes hesitation, and hesitation can cause
Your worst fears of all to come true.
And like most things in life, the actions you take
Have everything to do with you.

You won't be able to move forward on the outside
Until your "inside" allows you the freedom to move.
Find the source of your hesitation, look it square in the eye,
Then move forward with strength! Your life will improve!

THE INEVITABILITY OF CHANGE

"The greatest remedy in the world is change."
So say the great thinkers down through the ages.
It's also said that change is inevitable.
The subject, historically, has filled many pages.

Without change, as you know, there is no growth...
Collectively or personally. (Check your personal journal.)
It is change that brings us everything we want,
And the beginning of all change is always internal.

To go from place to place is not a change
Unless it produces a renewal of one's mind.
If you change the way you look at things,
The things you look at will change, you will find.

As Nelson Mandela is quoted for this wisdom
About the imperative need for education:
"Education is the most powerful weapon you can use
To change the world." (spoken with no hesitation)

The only human institution which rejects the idea
Of change is your local cemetery.
If you think it is not necessary to change,
You are thinking that survival is not really mandatory.

WILLIAM JAMES, YOU ARE SO WISE

Believe me, there are acts that are worth repeating,
By forming habits that serve all one's life –
Acts of kindness and honesty and caring,
Which are guaranteed to cut down the strife.

Positive habits bring positive results;
While negative habits bring negative, unequivocally.
The distance between the two is insurmountable.
Positive and negative do not act reciprocally.

The habit to avoid – the worst of the lot –
Is complacency or inaction. As James would envision
"There's no more miserable human being than one
In whom nothing is habitual but indecision."

A CLOSING THOUGHT

POETRY

It's the revelation
Of a sensation
That the poet
(Wouldn't you know it)
Believes to be
Felt only interiorly
And personal to
The writer who
... **writes it.**

It's the interpretation
Of a sensation
That was fueled by
A poet's sigh
And believed to be
Shared mutually
And personal to
The lucky one who
... **reads it.**

About the Author

Kathryn Carole Ellison is a former newspaper columnist
and journalist and, of course, a poet.

She lives near her children and stepchildren and their families in the
Pacific Northwest, and spends winters in the sunshine of Arizona.

You might find her on the golf course, traveling the world, writing poems,
or enjoying the arts in the company of dear friends.

Late Bloomer

Our culture honors youth with all
It's unbridled effervescence.
We older ones sit back and nod
As if in acquiescence.

And when our confidence really gels
In early convalescence...
"We can't be getting old!" we cry,
"We're still struggling with adolescence!"

Acknowledgments

I have many people to thank...

First of all, my (now) adult children, Jon and Nicole LaFollette, and Jon's wife Eva LaFollette, for inspiring the writing of the poems in the first place... and for encouraging me to continue writing poems, even though their wisdom and understanding, and their compassion, surpasses mine...

And thanks to the rest of my wonderful family that I inherited in 1985 when I married their father, Bill Ellison... Debbie Bacon, Jeff Ellison and Tom Ellison, and their respective spouses, John, Sandy and Sue. They, along with their children and grandchildren, are a major part of my daily living, and I am blessed to have them in my life.

Thank you, good friends, who have received poems of mine in Christmas cards over the years, for complimenting the messages in my poems.

Your encouragement helped to keep me writing and gave me the courage to publish.

I am indebted to Kim Kiyosaki who introduced me to the right person to get the publishing process under way... Mona Gambetta with Brisance Books Group has made the publishing process seem easy. I marvel at her abilities and her good humor, and treasure our friendship.

Thanks to Amy Anderson, Sonya Kopetz, Kerri Kazarba Schneider, and Ingrid Pape-Sheldon, my very first, most creative, public relations team of experts who have helped to carry my poems and my story to the world.

And... finally, thanks to John B. Laughlin, a fellow traveler in life, who encourages me every day in the writing and publishing process.

John, I love having you along for this magical ride.

BOOKS OF LIFE AND LOVE
by Kathryn Carole Ellison